I Love Sports
Hockey

by Allan Morey

Bullfrog Books

Ideas for Parents and Teachers

Bullfrog Books let children practice reading informational text at the earliest reading levels. Repetition, familiar words, and photo labels support early readers.

Before Reading

- Discuss the cover photo. What does it tell them?

- Look at the picture glossary together. Read and discuss the words.

Read the Book

- "Walk" through the book and look at the photos. Let the child ask questions. Point out the photo labels.

- Read the book to the child, or have him or her read independently.

After Reading

- Prompt the child to think more. Ask: Have you ever played hockey? Did you play on an indoor rink or outside on a lake or pond?

Bullfrog Books are published by Jump!
5357 Penn Avenue South
Minneapolis, MN 55419
www.jumplibrary.com

Library of Congress Cataloging-in-Publication Data

Morey, Allan.
 Hockey / by Allan Morey.
   pages cm. — (I love sports)
 Summary: "This photo-illustrated book for early readers introduces the basics of hockey and encourages kids to try it. Includes labeled diagram of hockey rink and photo glossary." — Provided by publisher.
 Includes index.
 Audience: Age: 5.
 Audience: Grade: K to Grade 3.
 ISBN 978-1-62031-180-6 (hardcover) —
 ISBN 978-1-62496-267-7 (ebook)
 1. Hockey for children—Juvenile literature. I. Title.
 GV848.6.C45H64 2015
 796.962—dc23
                                    2014032129

Series Editor: Rebecca Glaser
Series Designer: Ellen Huber
Book Designer: Anna Peterson
Photo Researcher: Jenny Fretland VanVoorst

Photo credits: All photos by Shutterstock except: Alamy, 24; Getty, 1, 3, 4, 10–11; Corbis, 5, 6–7, 9, 10–11, 12–13, 16–17, 18, 19; iStock, cover, 20–21; SuperStock 14–15.

Printed in the United States of America at Corporate Graphics in North Mankato, Minnesota.

Table of Contents

Let's Play Hockey! 4

At the Hockey Rink 22

Picture Glossary 23

Index 24

To Learn More 24

Let's Play Hockey!

Put on your ice skates.
Grab a hockey stick.

Let's play!

Tim is on one team.
Ben is on the other.
They get ready
to face off.

The puck drops.

puck

The game starts.

Lea has the puck.

She passes it.

It slides on the ice.

Kit gets it.

Josie swings her stick.

Crack!

The puck flies in the air.

It heads for the goal.

goal

glove ····▶

Sam is the goalie.

He has a big glove.

He catches the puck.

He makes a save.

Josie has the puck again.

She skates right.

She skates left.

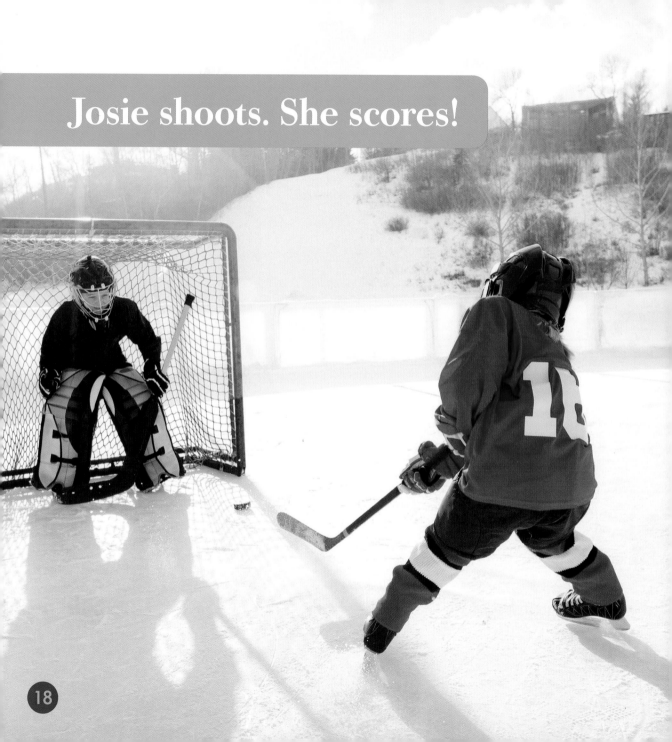

Josie shoots. She scores!

Now her team is ahead.

Do you want to play?
Grab your stick
and a puck.

Hockey is fun!

21

At the Hockey Rink

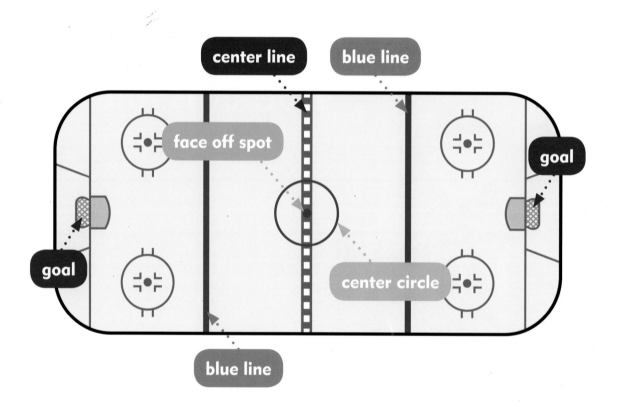

center line

blue line

face off spot

goal

goal

center circle

blue line

Picture Glossary

face off
To stand facing a player from the other team and try to get the puck first.

puck
A hard, black, rubber disc used somewhat like a ball to play hockey.

goalie
The player who tries to keep the other team from making a goal.

save
When a goalie stops the puck from going into the goal.

glove
A special piece of padded equipment that goalies wear to help them stop the puck.

team
A group of players who play together; there are 6 players on a hockey team.

Index

face off 7

glove 15

goal 13

goalie 15

ice skates 4

passing 11

puck 8, 11, 13, 15, 16, 21

save 15

stick 4, 13, 21

team 7, 19

To Learn More

Learning more is as easy as 1, 2, 3.

1) Go to www.factsurfer.com

2) Enter "hockey" into the search box.

3) Click the "Surf" button to see a list of websites.

With factsurfer.com, finding more information is just a click away.